Franz Joseph Haydn

Te Deum
for the Empress Marie Therese
(1800)

VOCAL SCORE

Edited by

DENIS McCALDIN

MUSIC DEPARTMENT

OXFORD
UNIVERSITY PRESS

OXFORD
UNIVERSITY PRESS

Great Clarendon Street, Oxford OX2 6DP
198 Madison Avenue, New York, NY10016, USA

Oxford University Press is a department of the University of Oxford
and furthers the University's aim of excellence in research, scholarship,
and education by publishing worldwide in

Oxford New York

Athens Auckland Bangkok Bogotá Buenos Aires Calcutta
Cape Town Chennai Dar es Salaam Delhi Florence Hong Kong Istanbul
Karachi Kuala Lumpur Madrid Melbourne Mexico City Mumbai
Nairobi Paris São Paulo Singapore Taipei Tokyo Toronto Warsaw

and associated companies in Berlin Ibadan

Oxford is a registered trademark of Oxford University Press

Full scores, vocal scores, and orchestral material
are available for hire from the publisher's hire library.

Scoring: flute, 2 oboes, 2 bassoons, 2 horns, 3 trumpets,
timpani, strings, organ, and mixed chorus.

Duration: *c.* 12 minutes

INTRODUCTION

When Haydn returned to Vienna from London in 1795 his reputation was as a celebrated composer of instrumental music. During the decade that followed he was to match that achievement with a remarkable series of vocal works which included not only the two late oratorios, *The Creation* and *The Seasons*, but also the six great Masses of 1796–1802 and this *Te Deum for the Empress Marie Therese*.

Among his most dedicated admirers during this period was the Empress Marie Therese, wife of Franz I of Austria. Musically gifted, she was particularly fond of singing, and Haydn was a frequent visitor at the Hofburg, the imperial palace in Vienna. He accompanied her 'pleasant but weak voice' on many occasions, including private performances of both *The Creation* and *The Seasons*. Their friendship led her to ask him repeatedly for some specially composed church music but Haydn's patron, Prince Nicolaus Esterhazy II, was very reluctant to allow his now famous Kapellmeister to write for anyone other than himself.

It seems likely that the Empress offered Haydn a particularly firm reminder of her request when she and her husband visited the Esterhazy estates in the summer of 1797 and that the composer delivered the *Te Deum* sometime thereafter. Extensive research in the Hofburg archives has failed to uncover the composer's autograph score or a set of contemporaneous parts which must now be presumed lost. No evidence is to be found there either concerning a première. The first authenticated performance was that directed by Haydn himself at Eisenstadt on 8 September 1800, the name-day of Prince Nicolaus' wife Princess Marie, during the visit by Lord Nelson and Lady Hamilton. This was the occasion when the D minor *Missa in angustiis* (now better known as the 'Nelson' Mass) was also heard.

Haydn composed two settings of the *Te Deum*; one in the 1760s, and this fine work from the latter period of his life. Both are in the key of C major and make extensive use of trumpets and drums, two features much associated with festive ceremony. This is also the tonality of many of the feast-day settings of the Mass which he would have sung as a chorister in St Stephen's Cathedral in Vienna. This later version of the *Te Deum*, though only 193 bars long, has a spacious grandeur which is impressive. It is in three contrasting sections. As in *The Creation*, with which it is roughly contemporary, C major and its minor tonality are shrewdly used to match the words. The opening paragraph 'Te deum laudamus' ('We praise thee, O God') in the tonic major is based on the Gregorian Eighth Psalm Tone. It relates in spirit to the vigorous affirmative style of 'The Heavens are telling' in the oratorio. In a similar way the darkness of the 'Representation of Chaos' is shared in the *Te Deum* at the words 'Te ergo quaesumus' ('We therefore pray thee help thy servants'). Musically, both sections share dark chromatic harmony and the sombre key of C minor. Haydn's respect for tradition has often been noted and in this work it is demonstrated by the chromatically descending bass line which looks back beyond the 'Crucifixus' of his own 'Little Organ Mass' to the many elegaic examples in church music of the baroque era. The final section marks a return to the optimism of the Resurrection and culminates in a fugue at the words 'In te speravi' ('Oh Lord, in Thee have I trusted'). Though this mood is momentarily upset by the dramatic appearance of a passage based on diminished sevenths at the words 'non confundar' ('let me never be confounded'), the final pages emphatically reaffirm Haydn's view of the unity of man with God in the celestial key of C major.

Among the more important revisions by Haydn which are included in this edition are the new tempo indications for both allegro sections; there are also some significant changes in dynamics and accentuation. Moreover, the Eisenstadt vocal parts show that he initially planned the work to begin at what is now bar nine, that is without the orchestral introduction, subsequently inserting a pause at the beginning of the choral scores to accomodate the instrumental prelude. In the light of this change, the later of the two sources in the Hofkapelle dated 1839 (Frühwald) has the following interesting comment: 'In the original, the eight bars indicated are presented at the outset as a ritornello, before the choral parts begin. These however are normally omitted in performance and so have not been written out at the opening.' There is no evidence that Haydn himself sanctioned this practice.

The piano reduction in this vocal score is based on the orchestral parts. Editorial suggestions have been made regarding ornamentation (bars 13 and 17). Generally speaking, Haydn's characteristic 'wedge' accent is equivalent to the modern staccato dot. Capitalization and punctuation of the text have been modernized. Although there are some syllabic slurs in the vocal parts of the sources, these are not consistent; in this vocal score they have been introduced throughout following modern practice. The critical edition of the full score gives full details on sources. All indications in square brackets and footnotes are editorial. Though conceived for smaller forces, the piece can be performed very successfully by choirs of more than 50 voices, providing that due care is taken to balance the orchestra.

Denis McCaldin
Lancaster/London, 1990

VORWORT

Als Haydn 1795 von London nach Wien zurückkehrte, wurde er vor allem als Komponist instrumentaler Musik gefeiert. Im folgenden Jahrzehnt sollte er jedoch vergleichbare Erfolge mit einer bemerkenswerten Reihe vokaler Werke erzielen, zu denen nicht nur die beiden späten Oratorien *Die Schöpfung* und *Die Jahreszeiten*, sondern auch die sechs großen Messen aus der Zeit von 1796 bis 1802 sowie sein *Te Deum für die Kaiserin Maria Theresia* zählten.

Die Kaiserin Maria Theresia, Gattin Franz I von Österreich, gehörte zu Haydns größten Bewunderern in dieser Zeit. Musikalisch begabt fand sie besonders am Singen Gefallen, und Haydn war ein häufiger Besucher der Hofburg, dem kaiserlichen Palast in Wien. Er begleitete ihr „angenehmes, aber schwaches Organ" bei vielen Gelegenheiten einschließlich privater Aufführungen der *Schöpfung* und der *Jahreszeiten*. Ihre Freundschaft veranlaßte die Kaiserin, Haydn wiederholt um speziell für sie komponierte Kirchenmusik zu bitten; Haydns Patron, Prinz Nikolaus Esterhazy II, erlaubte seinem inzwischen berühmten Kapellmeister jedoch nur ungern, für jemand anders als ihn selbst zu komponieren.

Es ist anzunehmen, daß die Kaiserin Haydn besonders deutlich an ihren Wunsch erinnerte, als sie mit ihrem Mann die Besitzungen Esterhazys im Sommer 1797 besuchte, und daß der Komponist irgendwann danach das *Te Deum* ablieferte. Selbst intensive Nachforschungen in den Archiven der Hofburg konnten die Originalpartitur des Komponisten oder einen zeitgenössischen Stimmensatz nicht zutage fördern, so daß sie nun als verschollen gelten müssen. Auch für eine Premiere gibt es keinerlei Zeugnis. Die erste nachgewiesene Aufführung dirigierte Haydn selbst am 8. September 1800, dem Namenstag von Prinz Nikolaus' Gattin Prinzessin Marie, in Eisenstadt während eines Besuchs von Lord Nelson und Lady Hamilton. Bei dieser Gelegenheit war auch die *Missa in angustiis* in d-moll (heute besser bekannt als die *Nelson-Messe*) zu hören.

Haydn vertonte das *Te Deum* zweimal: Die erste Fassung stammt aus den 1760er Jahren und die hier vorliegende zweite Fassung aus der letzten Lebensphase. Beide Vertonungen stehen in C-dur und machen häufigen Gebrauch von Trompeten und Pauken, zwei Merkmale, die oft mit festlichen Zeremonien in Verbindung gebracht werden. C-dur ist auch die Tonart vieler Festtagsvertonungen der Messe, die Haydn als Chorsänger in der St.-Stephan-Kathedrale in Wien gesungen haben dürfte. Die vorliegende spätere Fassung des *Te Deum* ist, obgleich nur 193 Takte lang, von einer prachtvollen Großzügigkeit, die beeindruckt. Sie besteht aus drei kontrastierenden Abschnitten. Wie in der *Schöpfung*, die etwa zur gleichen Zeit entstanden ist, werden C-dur und die gleichnamige Molltonart hier geschickt eingesetzt, um den Wortsinn zu unterstreichen. Der eröffnende Abschnitt „Te deum laudamus" („Großer Gott, wir loben dich") in der dur-Tonika basiert auf dem achten gregorianischen Psalmton. Im Charakter ähnelt er dem kraftvoll bejahenden Stil von „Die Himmel erzählen" des Oratoriums. In ähnlicher Weise läßt sich die Dunkelheit der „Vorstellung des Chaos" mit den Worten „Te ergo quaesumus" („Deshalb bitten wir dich um Hilfe") des *Te Deum* vergleichen. Musikalisch gesehen haben beide Abschnitte eine dunkle chromatische Harmonik und die düstere Tonart c-moll gemeinsam. Auf Haydns Achtung für die Tradition wurde oft hingewiesen. Ein Zeichen dafür ist in diesem Werk die chromatisch absteigende Baßlinie, die noch über den „Cruxifixus" seiner eigenen *Kleinen Orgelmesse* hinaus auf die vielen elegischen Beispiele in barocker Kirchenmusik zurückweist. Im Schlußteil findet eine Rückkehr zum Optimismus der Auferstehung statt, wobei der Höhepunkt in einer Fuge bei den Worten „In te, speravi" („Auf dich habe ich vertraut") erreicht wird. Obwohl diese Stimmung vorübergehend durch eine dramatische Passage, die bei den Worten „non confundar" („verdamme mich nicht") auf verminderten Septimen basiert, getrübt wird, bestätigen die Schlußseiten nachdrücklich Haydns Vorstellung von der Einheit des Menschen mit Gott in der „himmlischen" Tonart C-dur.

Zu den wichtigeren Revisionen Haydns, die in dieser Ausgabe enthalten sind, gehören die neuen Tempo-Bezeichnungen in beiden allegro-Abschnitten; auch gibt es einige deutliche Veränderungen im Bereich der Dynamik und Akzentuierung. Zudem läßt sich aus den Eisenstädter Vokalstimmen ersehen, daß Haydn ursprünglich die Absicht hatte, das Werk dort zu beginnen, wo sich jetzt Takt 9 befindet, also ohne Orchestereinleitung. In der Folge fügte er eine Pause vor dem Einsatz der Chorstimmen ein, um das instrumentale Vorspiel voranstellen zu können. Die spätere der beiden Quellen in der Hofkapelle, die aus dem Jahre 1839 (Frühwald) datiert, enthält einen angesichts obiger Änderung besonders interessanten Kommentar: „Im Originale sind im Anfange — bevor die Singstimmen eintreten — die hier beyschriebenen 8 Takte als Ritornell; welche aber bey Productionen gewohnlich ausgelassen werden und darum Anfangs gar nicht geschrieben wurden." Es ist nicht belegt, daß Haydn dieses Verfahren guthieß.

Der Klavierauszug in der Chorpartitur basiert auf den Orchesterstimmen. Vorschläge des Herausgebers zu den Verzierungen (Takt 13 und 17) sind enthalten. Im allgemeinen sind die charakteristischen Akzente Haydns als gleichbedeutend mit dem modernen staccato-Punkt zu verstehen. Großschreibung und Zeichensetzung des Textes wurden modernisiert. Es gibt zwar einige syllabische Bindebögen in den Vokalstimmen der Quellen, diese erscheinen jedoch nicht konsequent. In der vorliegenden Chorpartitur wurden sie gemäß heutiger Praxis durchgehend ergänzt. In der Kritischen Ausgabe der Partitur sind vollständige Einzelheiten über die Quellen enthalten. Alle Angaben in eckigen Klammern und Fußnoten stammen vom Herausgeber.

Obwohl das Werk ursprünglich für eine große Besetzung gedacht war, kann es auch sehr erfolgreich von kleineren Chören aufgeführt werden, vorausgesetzt, es wird ein entsprechendes Gleichgewicht mit dem Orchester hergestellt.

Übersetzung: Petra Woodfull-Harris

Denis McCaldin
Lancaster/London, 1990

Te Deum

for the Empress Marie Therese

Edited by Denis McCaldin

FRANZ JOSEPH HAYDN (1732–1809)
Hob. XXIIIc: 2

Allegro con spirito

* See Introduction

* Sung
Se - ra -

* Played ♩♩♩♩ throughout

32

Sa - ba - oth. Ple - ni sunt cae - li et ter - ra

Sa - ba - oth. Ple - ni sunt cae - li et ter - ra

Sa - ba - oth. Ple - ni sunt cae - li et ter - ra

Sa - ba - oth. Ple - ni sunt cae - li et ter - ra

35

ma - je - sta - tis glo - ri - ae tu -

ma - je - sta - tis glo - ri - ae tu -

ma - je - sta - tis glo - ri - ae tu -

ma - je - sta - tis glo - ri - ae tu -

61

Patris sem-pi-ter - nus es Fi - li - us.

Patris sem-pi-ter - nus es Fi - li - us.

Patris sem-pi - ter - nus es Fi - li-us. Tu ad li-be-ran-dum

Patris sem-pi-ter - nus es Fi - li-us. Tu ad li-be-ran - dum

64

non hor-ru-i - sti Vir - gi-nis u - te-rum.

non hor-ru-i - sti Vir - gi-nis u - te-rum.

sus-cep-tu-rus ho - mi-nem,

sus-cep-tu-rus ho - mi-nem,

* Sung

Tu de - vic - to mor - tis a - cu - le - o,

a - pe - ru - i - sti, a - pe - ru - i - sti cre -

71

-den - ti - bus re - gna cae - lo - rum.

-den - ti - bus re - gna cae - lo - rum.

-den - ti - bus re - gna cae - lo - rum.

-den - ti - bus re - gna cae - lo - rum.

74

Tu ad dex - te - ram De - i se - des, in

Tu ad dex - te - ram De - i se - des, in

Tu ad dex - te - ram De - i se - des, in

Tu ad dex - te - ram De - i se - des, in_

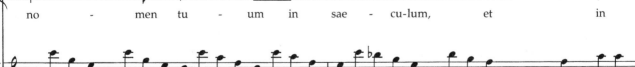

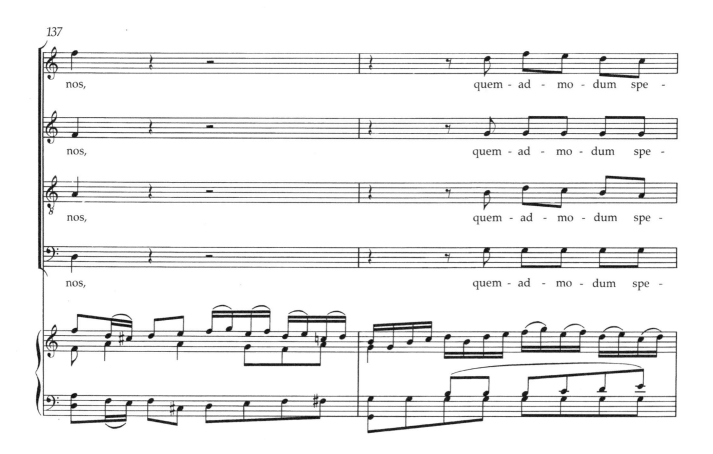

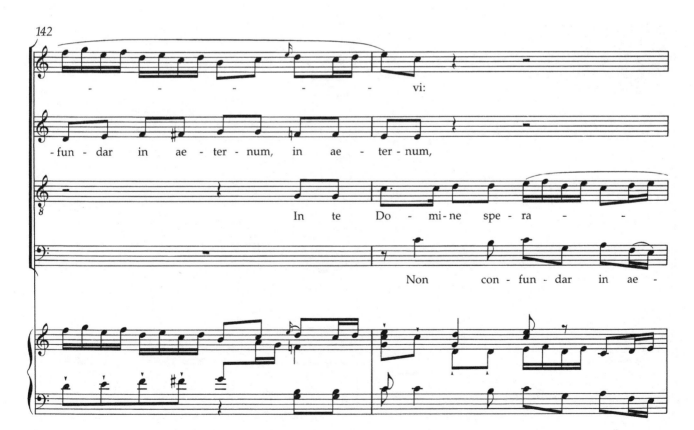

non con - fun - dar in ae -

non con - fun - dar in ae - ter - num,

- - - - - - vi: non con - fun - dar

- ter - num, in ae - ter - num, in ae - ter - num, non con - fun - dar

- ter - num, in ae - ter - num,

in te Do - mi - ne spe - ra - -

in ae - ter - num, non con - fun - dar, non con -

in ae - ter - num, in ae - ter - num,

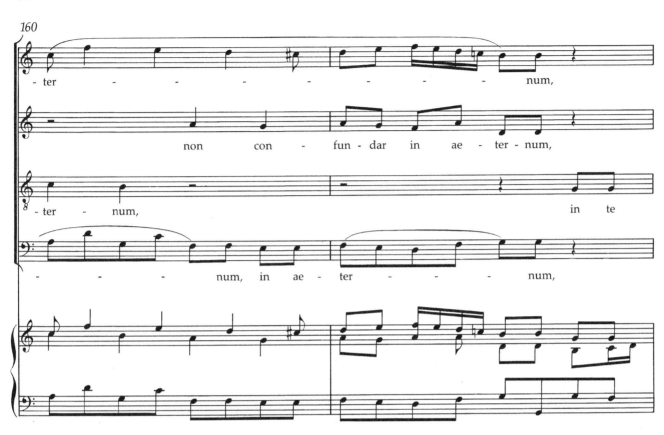

in ae - ter - num, non con-fun-dar in ae - ter-num, non con-fun-dar in ae -

in ae - ter - num, non con-fun-dar in ae - ter-num, non con-fun-dar in ae -

in ae - ter - num, non con-fun-dar in ae - ter-num, non con-fun-dar in ae -

in ae - ter - num, non con-fun-dar in ae - ter-num, non con-fun-dar in ae -

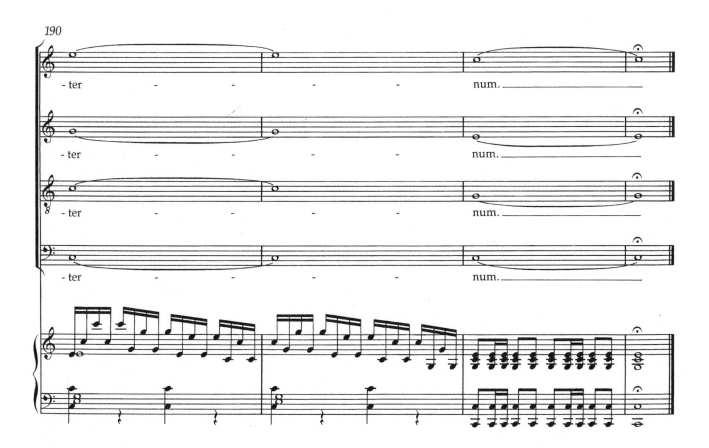

- ter - - - - num. _____

- ter - - - - num. _____

- ter - - - num. _____

- ter - - - num. _____